Praise for Sex

"With its hilarious and helpful challenges, this fun little book packs a powerful punch! It's refreshing to see a sexual self-help book that's accessible to everyone."
—Karen Salmansohn, bestselling author of How to Be Happy, Dammit and The Clitourist

"As a sexual health consultant, my clients need opportunities to increase sexual communication, and Sexy Slang's new book and games are the perfect solution! With a little imagination and creativity, couples play their way straight to the bedroom."
—Andrea Adams-Miller, relationship and intimacy specialist, author, and SexTalk LIVE! radio show host

"My husband (Carter Evans of CNN) and I are big fans of Sexy Slang! It is hysterical and from the first time we played, we were hooked!"
—Courtney Friel, Fox News correspondent

"As a talk show host who mainly deals in the love and dating realm, one of the biggest problems I hear from my listeners is, 'My relationship has fallen flat.' With Sexy Slang, couples can tackle not only their communication issues but break their boundaries to reach a new level of intimacy. Genius!"
—Diana Falzone, host of Cosmo Radio's Cosmolicious

SEXY SLANG'S
Bedroom
Challenges

SEXY SLANG'S
Bedroom
Challenges

69 WAYS TO SPICE UP YOUR SEX LIFE

Christi Smith Scofield and Ted Scofield

sourcebooks
casablanca

Copyright © 2010 by Christi Smith Scofield and Ted Scofield
Cover and internal illustrations © PFF Entertainment, LLC
Cover and internal illustrations by Melanie Taylor, T. C. Russell, Redjing Calma, Justine Galvez, Cristina Martinez Byvik
Cover design by William Riley/Sourcebooks

Published by Sourcebooks Casablanca, an imprint of Sourcebooks, Inc.
P.O. Box 4410, Naperville, Illinois 60567-4410
(630) 961-3900
Fax: (630) 961-2168
www.sourcebooks.com

Library of Congress Cataloging-in-Publication Data

Scofield, Christi Smith.
  Sexy Slang's bedroom challenges : 69 ways to spice up your sex life / by Christi Smith Scofield and Ted Scofield.
    p. cm.
  1. Sexual excitement. 2. Sexual intercourse. 3. Sex instruction. I. Scofield, Ted. II. Title.
  HQ31.S376 2010
  306.77--dc22

                              2010010673

              Printed and bound in the United States of America.
                   SP 10 9 8 7 6 5 4 3 2 1

To our parents,
who taught us the value of open,
honest communication

Contents

Acknowledgments

We'd like to thank our families for their unconditional love and support, particularly our amazing parents. Special thanks to our fabulous editor, Shana Drehs, and our dedicated agent, Krista Goering, both of whom loved this book from the beginning, and to our amazing chief navigation officer, Michelle Patterson, who helped us tremendously in preparing for the launch. Without our talented artists, this book would not have been possible. Thank you, T.C.R., Melanie Taylor, Cristina Martinez Byvik, Redjing Calma, and Justine Galvez. Finally, we're thrilled to give a shout out to PFF Entertainment's loyal investors, without whom our company would not exist, much less this book.

One final thanks to our partners and sponsors whose amazing products and advice we highly recommend. **Please visit our site www.sexyslang.com/bedroomchallenges.html to see special offers from our sponsors to you, our readers.**

Introduction

Have you ever wanted to bring up a topic in the bedroom but felt awkward doing so? Have you looked for ways to break the ice when it comes to potentially taboo subjects? If so, *Sexy Slang's Bedroom Challenges* is perfect for you. This book offers a playful and unintimidating way to introduce sexual dialogue and new ideas into your relationship.

By exploring body parts, toys, positions, and everything in between, we will get you talking about sexual topics that you thought you would never be able to discuss with your partner, much less actually try! Each topic offers a new his or her challenge that can help open up communication with your lover in a fun, lighthearted way.

In 2008, we launched the Sexy Slang board game, best described as a mix of Pictionary and charades, but with 500 naughty terms. Within weeks of the game's launch, fans amazed us with stories about how playing the game had opened up opportunities for them to talk to their lovers and spouses about sexual topics that were normally difficult to discuss or were even left unspoken. If a game can have such a positive impact on people's relationships, we asked ourselves, imagine what a book could do? You will soon find out!

In keeping with the fun, lighthearted mood of our Sexy Slang games and other products, we created *Sexy Slang's Bedroom Challenges* so that it captures some of the exciting play found in our Sexy Slang board game. The challenges will have you laughing as you and your lover guess the Sexy Slang pictograms, try your hand at describing them, and answer insightful questions. Don't worry; it's not an inquisition. Most of the questions don't have a wrong answer. Our goal is to make sure you win that BOOTY PRIZE as often as possible!

You'll find that some of the pictograms are more challenging than others, and some of the terms aren't exactly slang. That's okay. We've included topics that we believe are important for couples to discuss, and we're confident you'll have a great time doing so.

So why not loosen up, have fun, and put some "vajayjay" into your vocabulary? (If you're not sure what that means, just keep reading.) *Sexy Slang's Bedroom Challenges* is the perfect book to allow you to laugh and lighten the mood while getting closer to your lover. Enjoy!

How to Use This Book

Sexy Slang's Bedroom Challenges contains 69 his-and-her challenges covering a wide variety of sexual topics. Each challenge poses three questions that must be answered to "score" the challenge's **BOOTY PRIZE**.

Without a doubt, some of the topics are more risqué than others. If you're not comfortable with a topic, feel free to skip it. We've included a wide range of challenges based on feedback we've received from Sexy Slang fans.

Start with chapter 1 or with whatever topic turns you on. Play a game with your lover as you attempt to guess the term represented by the Sexy Slang pictogram and then try to define it. Not all of the terms are strictly slang, and not all of the pictograms are particularly difficult to guess, but we think you'll enjoy them nonetheless.

Flip the page to read some fun facts and titillating tidbits about the topic, and then learn more about each other as you answer three questions that relate to it. Celebrate your newfound knowledge with the BOOTY PRIZE!

Guess the term…

Define it if you can…

Read the fun facts…

Answer the questions…

Celebrate with the BOOTY PRIZE!

HER CHALLENGES
She guesses what Sexy Slang term the pictogram represents, tries to define the term, and answers the questions. He reads the page to her and delivers the BOOTY PRIZE.

HIS CHALLENGES
He guesses, tries to define the Sexy Slang term, and answers the questions. She reads the page to him and delivers the BOOTY PRIZE.

WHERE TO BEGIN?
Start at the beginning of the book, or open to any pictogram. If you're searching for something specific, you'll see that the chapters are organized into broad categories. For example, if you're game for "a walk on the wild side," go directly to chapter 8.

Sexy Slang's Bedroom Challenges is designed to be "interactive." We suggest keeping the book on a nightstand or in your goodie drawer (see chapter 7 if you don't know what that term means), somewhere it is easily accessible when the need "arises." (Pardon the pun.)

Most importantly, **have fun!** If a topic is too intimidating for either of you or simply not your cup of tea, move on. *Sexy Slang's Bedroom Challenges* contains topics and challenges for all levels of sexual experience. What one reader finds offensive, another may find ho-hum. Our goal is to entertain and educate, but if you're not comfortable with a featured sexual practice or subject matter, skip to the next one.

The goal of *Sexy Slang's Bedroom Challenges* is to break down the barriers of bedroom communication. To do so, you must…communicate. Talk, laugh, blush, moan, sigh…wink, wiggle, whisper. **Be open and honest with each other. That is the true challenge, and we hope you succeed.**

Hooters,
Hoohas,
and More

1

Sell your books at
sellbackyourBook.com!
Go to sellbackyourBook.com
and get an instant price quote.
We even pay the shipping - see
what your old books are worth
today!

Inspected By:armandina_rios

00033777867

G

7867

0003377

☐ HOOTERS

☐ **Definition:** Breasts, more often called boobs, knockers, jugs, melons, sweater puffs, the girls, and, last but not least, the twins.

☐ **Does she have a name for her bosom buddies?**

☐ **What is her favorite bra? What do you think is the sexiest type of bra? "None" is not an answer!**

☐ **Does a trip to second base turn her on?**

> **FUN FACTS!**
> *The twins vary tremendously in shape and size. Just like Thelma was taller than Louise, the left boob is usually slightly larger than the right on most women.* ♂

Breasts are an excellent seduction tool. Show that cleavage, girl! Fondling breasts can be great foreplay. They are sensitive to your touch, boys, so remember to stroke and nibble lightly until you know how much pressure she likes. If you are a man who likes to squeeze, approach breasts like they are water balloons rather than stress balls.

BOOTY PRIZE!
One 5-minute session of sweater-puff fondling.

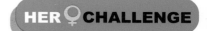

☐ HEADLIGHTS

☐ **Definition:** Also known as high beams, peanuts, or smuggling raisins, headlights occur when the girls are standing at full attention. In more clinical terms, the nipples are erect.

☐ **Are your nipples an erogenous zone?**

☐ **What about his? Does he like to have his stimulated?**

☐ **What do you like best? Stroking, licking, sucking, pinching, nibbling, or what else?**

FUN FACTS!
Is she really happy to see you? Not necessarily. Nipples contain hundreds of nerves and muscle fibers that contract when the temperature drops or even if her clothes rub a certain way. Headlights don't always indicate that she is aroused, but for men it can be a turn-on just to speculate.

When going for the nip, be sure to dive in gently. Nipple sensitivity varies from person to person. Test slowly with a variety of techniques: blowing, caressing, teasing, and squeezing. If you find one pleasurable, perhaps branch out with accoutrements like ice cubes, honey, or whipped cream.

BOOTY PRIZE!
One foreplay session comprised solely of headlight stimulation.

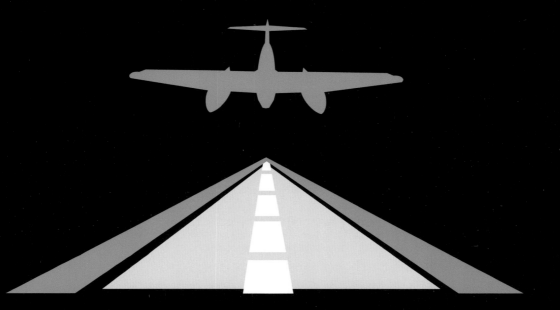

☐ LANDING STRIP

☐ **Definition:** A hooha hairstyle. The pubic hair is removed until only a narrow, vertical rectangle of hair remains. Make sure it's a soft landing, fly boy!

☐ **Do you like your kitty long haired, short haired, or hairless?**

☐ **Would you like for me to try out something new down under?**

☐ **Which grooming habits of mine turn you on? Perfume? Shampoo? Smooth legs? Pedicures?**

FUN FACTS!
A Brazilian bikini wax usually leaves a landing strip. However, it takes grooming to the next level by pulling up the carpet, from the labia majora down to the perineum and the bum. A Hollywood wax, also referred to as the Sphinx, is when you take it all off. ♂

Staying well-groomed is hard work and sometimes even painful. If you are not ready to head to the salon to throw your heels over head for a perfect stranger, you do have other options. Quite a few do-it-yourself home-waxing kits are available, or for something a little less masochistic, go for a personal-grooming shaver.

BOOTY PRIZE:
One personal-grooming session with your lover.
Who grooms who is up to you!

☐ BEAVER

☐ **Definition:** A vajayjay, cootchie, honey pot, bearded clam, love canal, whisker biscuit...you get the picture.

☐ **Which part of your lady business is the most sensitive?**

☐ **Do you like a deep thrust or circular motions?**

☐ **Have you ever tried to exercise your love grotto?**

> **FUN FACTS!**
> *A vagina generally measures between 3 and 6 inches with the average being 4.5 inches. When the vagina is not aroused, its walls are closed together like a flattened tube, but when it's aroused, look out! It's made of muscles that can expand, contract, and really grip his stick.*

Get fit, girls! Kegel exercises, which contract and release the pubococcygeus (PC) muscles found in the hooha, are a great way to enhance your sexual pleasure and increase the intensity of your orgasms.

If you don't know your PCs from your pectorals, not to worry. An easy way to find them is to visit the powder room and take a tinkle. Stop midstream, then start again, and then stop again. If you can do that, you have found the PC muscles and can repeat the exercises anywhere (no tinkling required). A suggested workout session is 20 reps, pausing and relaxing the muscles in between.

BOOTY PRIZE
Thirty minutes of beaver love. Method? Her choice.
(But beavers are known to love wood.)

☐ LITTLE MAN IN THE BOAT

☐ **Definition:** The clitoris. Also known as the love button, the bean, and the on-switch.

☐ **Do you know how to find the little man in the boat?**

☐ **Do you know what to do when you find it?**

☐ **Would you like a lesson on this fantastic little joy buzzer?**

> **FUN FACTS!**
> *The clitoris is the only human organ with sexual pleasure as its only known function!*

Like the male tallywhacker, the clitoris swells with blood and grows in size when aroused. As most women happily know, it is the most sensitive of the erogenous zones, with thousands of nerve endings (twice as many as in a trouser snake). Stimulating this little love nub is the most common—and sometimes the only—way to bring a woman to orgasm.

BOOTY PRIZE
Watch her turn on and get off by pushing the love button.
Who does the pushing is up to you.

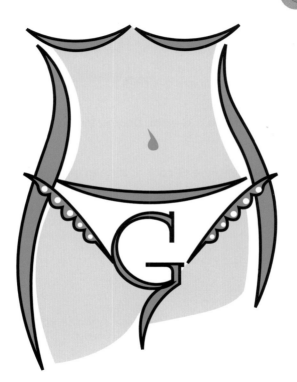

☐ G-SPOT

☐ **Definition:** The Gräfenberg spot is located about 2 inches inside the front wall of the vagina. For some women, it offers another "fountain" of female pleasure. For others, it is much ado about nothing.

☐ **Studies say that not all women have a G-spot. Do you think you have one?**

☐ **Shall we try to find it together?**

☐ **What turns you on more? Touching the G-spot or stimulating the clitoris?**

GPS to the G-spot: It's easier to find when she's excited. Insert one finger into the vajayjay, and bend the finger upwards as if you're beckoning her to come hither. The spot should feel spongy, with a rough surface similar to corrugated cardboard or a walnut. As with all new explorations, proceed carefully and gently. If she responds with a moan, then you know you have arrived at your destination.

BOOTY PRIZE

Show off your multitasking skills, boys! Find the G-spot and the little man in the boat, and stimulate them simultaneously.

☐ JUNK IN THE TRUNK

☐ **Definition:** An ample posterior. Also referred to as bootylicious.

☐ **Do you like a little more gear in the rear, or are you a skinny-butt guy?**

☐ **Thong, boy shorts, or granny panties? Lace or cotton?**

☐ **What item of clothing best complements my beautiful bum?**

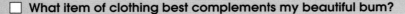

FUN FACTS!
If your loins stir at the sight of a healthy tush, you may be a pygophilist. Pygophilia is sexual excitement caused by seeing, touching, or fondling a woman's derrière.

The gluteals are huge muscles and can benefit from regular massage, especially if you exercise. A proper butt massage is both relaxing and erotic. Touching and massaging the bum can create excitement through anticipation as you work your way to other "amorous" areas.

BOOTY PRIZE
One 10-minute butt massage.
Who knows what will come next?

Trouser Snakes and Stepchildren

2

HIS ♂ CHALLENGE

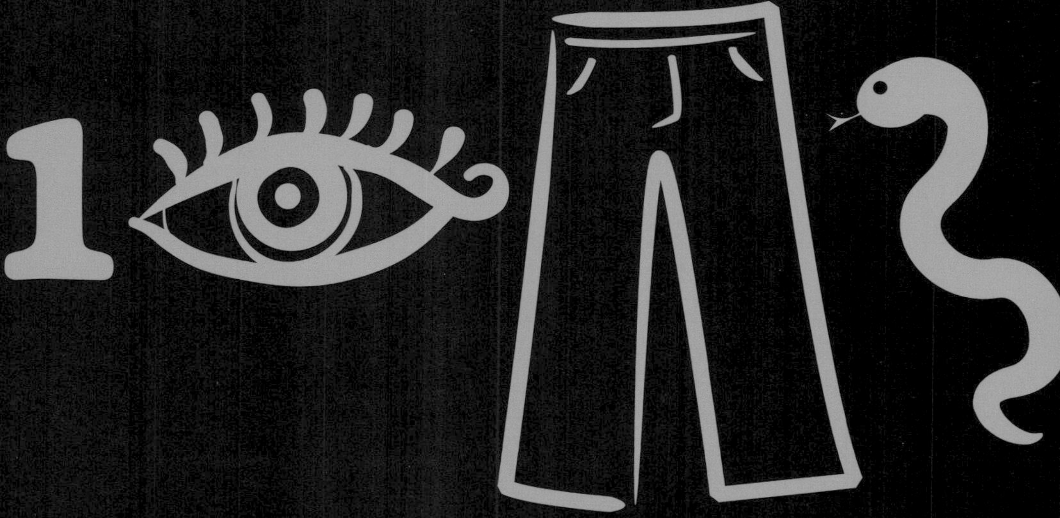

ONE-EYED TROUSER SNAKE

Definition: The male organ of copulation, more widely known as the penis, johnson, willy, pecker, schlong, heat-seeking moisture missile, or tallywhacker. A small one is a schmeckel; a big one's a third leg. Whatever the case may be, ladies, remember that his is always perfect.

What is your favorite name for your trouser snake?

Have you ever had a "wardrobe malfunction" with your member? Was it really a malfunction?

Would you consider yourself a grower or a show-er?

The head of the penis, otherwise known as the glans, is full of nerve endings. The most sensitive part is called the frenulum, that v-shaped area on the underside of the johnson where the shaft meets the head. Ladies, be sure to pay special attention to this pleasure zone. A little frenulum fondling can work wonders.

BOOTY PRIZE
One 5-minute session of fondling fun!

☐ MANSCAPING

☐ **Definition:** Male body grooming. Many people think this term means hair removal below the belt, but in fact, it means hair removal in all areas of the body, including the back, ears, nose, neck, groin, and bum. All areas of the body are fair game, including his "boys."

☐ **How do you feel about male body hair?**

☐ **On what area of your boy toy would you like to see less or more?**

☐ **What part of his current grooming regimen do you like best? Cologne? A close shave? Fresh breath?**

When manscaping below the belt, men should take care in trimming sensitive areas. If you're just getting started and looking to make a forest into a topiary, begin with scissors but finish up with a trimmer or razor for a more even look. If you are "ballsy," you can go for a "manzilian." Just like a woman's Brazilian, wax is applied all the way from your front to the back and everywhere in between, including the jewels. Let 'er rip!

BOOTY PRIZE
Gentlemen, start your trimmers. Ladies, it's your choice.
Pick an area that you would like to see manscaped.

WELL HUNG

- **Definition:** To be well endowed.
- **Women's Definition:** 8 inches.
- **Men's Definition:** 3 inches.
- Have you ever experienced "shrinkage" at an inopportune moment?
- What's your favorite thing about your beef thermometer?
- What do you think my favorite thing is about your erotic python of love?

> **FUN FACTS!**
> *Free that big willy! The largest penis measured in the world belongs to the blue whale, which sports a monstrous 10 footer. The human record is a "mere" 13.5 inches. Not to fret, boys. The average size is actually 5.5 inches, and that's when it's standing at attention.*

Good news, boys! Eighty-five percent of women are satisfied with their partners' johnsons. Most women say that skill beats out size any day, and since the average hooha is only 3 to 5 inches long, any length above the average really goes to waste. Remember that the first third of a woman's pink velvet sausage wallet contains most of the nerve endings, so you don't need to be a giant to get the job done. Use the tools you have, and use them well!

BOOTY PRIZE
Make it happen, ladies! Get that grower to show or that show-er to grow!

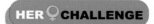

☐ WOODY

☐ **Definition:** Boner, chubby, stiffy, pitching a tent, morning glory, rigid digit, throbbing thrill hammer, or, in clinical terms, an erection.

☐ **How often do you think your man sports wood in an average day?**

☐ **Have you ever seen or caused him to experience an inappropriate boner?**

☐ **Does he ever have a morning glory? Have you taken advantage of it?**

The baloney pony does have a mind all its own. The same part of a man's autonomic nervous system that keeps him breathing and his heart pumping is also responsible for him pitching a tent. Most woodies are caused by sexual arousal; however, something as simple as the wind blowing can get the little general to stand at attention. That's why he's always carrying his briefcase in front.

BOOTY PRIZE
Batter up, boys! You've waited a whole 4 paragraphs.
It's time to give her some good wood!

☐ FAMILY JEWELS

☐ **Definition:** Testicles. Also referred to as nuts, stones, cojones, berries, stepchildren, happy sacks, or just your basic…balls.

☐ **Do your stepchildren get enough attention?**

☐ **How do you like them to be loved? Touching? Squeezing? Licking? Sucking?**

☐ **Which one of yours hangs lower? Let's have a look, shall we?**

How to know and love his boys? One word: gently.
These puppies are super sensitive, but stimulation can provide a very erotic sensation for him. Don't ignore the happy sacks, but always tread lightly as you try new things. If you are yanking and tugging, those might not be screams of ecstasy you hear.

BOOTY PRIZE

One step-by-step lesson on the proper care and handling of the crown jewels.

☐ CHOCOLATE STARFISH

☐ **Definition:** The bum hole, the back door, the balloon knot. It's your rear exit, and yes, if you haven't already discovered this, it's also a possible entrance.

☐ **What do you think of my buns?**

☐ **Do you know how to find the perineum?**

☐ **How do you feel about touching the starfish?**

FUN FACTS!
According to the National Survey of Family Growth, 34 percent of men and 30 percent of women reported engaging in back-door sexual activity at least once.

Massaging the "G" for the big "O" is not just for the ladies. Men also have a G-spot. It's called the prostate gland, and it's an amazing sexual weapon. About the size of a chestnut, it's located about 2 inches inside the back door on the front wall and contains some sensitive nerve endings. Some men might have an issue with rear-entry play, but not to fear. There is nothing more hetero than having your girl stimulate you to a mind-blowing G-spot "O."

BOOTY PRIZE
One session of "tainted love."
Since both of you have a perineum, the recipient of this love is up to her.

Start Me
Up

3

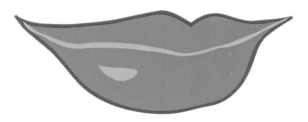

☐ LOCK LIPS

☐ **Definition:** Smooching, sucking face, macking, snogging, getting to first base, or just plain kissing.

☐ How do you feel about locking lips in public (PDA, public displays of affection)?

☐ When did you have your first kiss? What do you remember about the experience?

☐ What type of kisses do you like? Wet and wild? Soft and dry? Lots of tongue?

> **FUN FACTS!**
> *Stressed out? Then it's time to make out! Kissing is a known stress reliever. It relieves tension, increases blood flow to the heart, and triggers the release of the feel-good hormone oxytocin. And, as a special bonus, snogging also burns calories!*

A good smooch session is an integral part of foreplay for many women. Not only is it very intimate, but the lips are also an erogenous zone. But don't just stick to the lips! Kissing all parts of her body is a great way to get her motor running.

BOOTY PRIZE
One kissing session that starts with a lip-lock and ends wherever he chooses or when she is begging for more than his lips.

☐ HEAVY PETTING

☐ **Definition:** Think of it as batting a triple: you touch every base without hitting a home run. Or, in other words, some serious hot and heavy foreplay.

☐ **Do you like a lot of petting, or do you just want to dive in for the real deal?**

☐ **Have you ever had an "incident" during a clothed session of heavy petting? No? Even when you were a teenager?**

☐ **On what parts of your body, other than Mr. Winkie, do you like to be petted?**

Foreplay in public? Sure! Not all foreplay has to start with touching. In fact, a great way to get in the mood is just to start thinking about sex. Next time you are out to dinner or at a party, whisper something hot into your lover's ear and get him or her thinking about the boudoir hours before you get there.

BOOTY PRIZE

Drive him crazy with some public petting and breathy banter. Continue until you arrive at a location where no indecency laws will be broken (or at least where you won't get caught). When he can no longer endure your torturous titillation, offer him a happy ending. But remember, it's "everything but!"

☐ SECOND BASE

☐ **Definition:** Getting a little boobage, fondling the twins, touching the tatas.

☐ **What's your favorite second-base play? Caressing, kissing, nibbling, licking, tweaking, circling, kneading, or what else?**

☐ **Rekindle fond memories. When did your boy toy first get to meet the twins?**

☐ **Have you ever teased or titillated your man with your tatas? Have you ever received a motorboat?**

Massaging the melons is not only sexually arousing but also good for the girls. A breast massage helps her to relax as well as reduces fibroids and cysts. Remember, when doing so, be gentle. Use a massage oil, and start by applying it in circular motions.

BOOTY PRIZE
One tender, hot, and sexy boob massage.

☐ HAPPY TRAIL

☐ **Definition:** Also known as the treasure trail. Follow this thin line of hair from his belly button to his pelvic region to unleash Mr. Happy.

FUN FACTS!
The anticipation a man builds during foreplay actually makes his orgasms more intense.

☐ **Do you like it when I follow the happy trail and touch all around the top of your boxers?**

☐ **What about your thighs?**

☐ **What are your other hot erogenous zones?**

Although men seem to want to dive right into the final act, most of them enjoy some sort of foreplay. Taking the time to seduce and touch every area except Mr. Happy is the perfect prelude to a mind-blowing main event.

BOOTY PRIZE
Twenty minutes of full-court-press seduction methods before visiting Mr. Johnson's neighborhood.

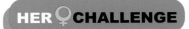

the

☐ TICKLE THE TACO

☐ **Definition:** Petting the kitty, getting to third base, stroking the lady business, or more clinically, stimulation of the female genitalia with one's hands.

☐ **Instead of going directly to third base, what should I do first?**

☐ **Can you put my hand on your favorite spots?**

☐ **Which direction should I rub? Should I dial zero on the pink telephone?**

FUN FACTS!
Women need about 20 minutes of foreplay to reach full arousal. Hello? Gentlemen? Women need about 20 minutes of foreplay to reach full arousal.

Foreplay begins in a woman's brain. Although men should be applauded for searching out and stimulating her joy buzzer, there are many ways to get a woman heated up. Women love the tease. Before you dive right in to tickle the taco, try caressing areas all around her body. When you get to the rosebud, touch gently all around to find the areas that she responds to best. Every woman is different. Part of the fun is finding her hot spots!

BOOTY PRIZE
Twenty minutes of moan-inducing precoital pleasure for her, only 10 of which can be spent stroking the lady business.

the

☐ TICKLE THE PICKLE

☐ **Definition:** Giving him a little hand relief, wrestling his eel, massaging the member or, more basically, a good old hand-job.

☐ **Do you prefer lube or lotion when your pickle is tickled, or au natural?**

☐ **What motion feels best? Hard or soft? Fast or slow?**

☐ **What should I do with my other hand? Pleasure the perineum? Or do the stepchildren crave some attention?**

Tickling the pickle need not be just a basic up-and-down, ho-hum exercise. You can reverse your grip for a totally different sensation or interweave your fingers. The key is communication. If you can't discern from his response what feels good and what doesn't, ask him! Oh, and don't forget the frenulum!

BOOTY PRIZE
Loosen up those fingers, ladies! He gets a 10-minute tickling session (but don't be surprised if it only lasts for 2!).

☐ JOY JELLY

☐ **Definition:** Artificial sexual lubrication, or just plain lube. It comes in a dizzying array of options: water-based, silicone-based, oil-based, heat-activated, scented, flavored, glow-in-the-dark…you get the drift.

☐ **Do you want to try it?**

☐ **What kind? Flavored for some tasty oral action? Wet and wild for some crazy carnal slip 'n' slide?**

☐ **How about a sensual "pleasure enhancement" lube that heats up and tingles when applied?**

> **FUN FACTS!**
> *If you are using a love glove, then keep the oil-based lubes for your next back massage. Use water- or silicone-based lubes with condoms since oil can eat away at Mr. Happy's raincoat.*

The wetter, the better! Lube can be an excellent addition to your sexual repertoire. Do not think of it as a sexual aid for something that is lacking but as a great way to enhance what you have. Even if she has plenty of natural lubrication, the addition of a water-based lube can allow for more long-lasting and vigorous love making. And even if you are dripping with anticipation, a flavored or heat-activated lube can add excitement and variation to your normal routine. So lube it up, baby!

BOOTY PRIZE

One erotic shopping spree for the lube of her choice. He's paying!
(If you're intimidated or confused by all the options, we've suggested a couple of our favorites at www.sexyslang.com/bedroomchallenges.html.)

Let's Talk about Sex

4

☐ HOT BEEF INJECTION

☐ **Definition:** Insertion of the man's hot salami into the woman's hooha. Bumping uglies, doing the mattress dance, knocking boots, sex.

☐ **How often would you like receive an "injection"?**

☐ **Shall we create a code word for sex that we can use in public?**

☐ **If you could bump uglies anywhere in the world, where would it be?**

Many couples disagree on how often they should knock boots. Issues and responsibilities such as work stress, children, lack of time, and fatigue can affect desire. Communicate with your partner about how often you would like sex and work together to find a happy medium. Find creative ways to overcome issues that are keeping desires at bay.
If you seem to never have enough time for sex, then make use of that new code word by placing it on your weekly (daily?) calendar. If you are just not in the mood, try thinking sexy thoughts, fantasizing, reading sexy books, or watching sexy movies. Never underestimate the power of sexual thinking!

BOOTY PRIZE
She's looking a little pale. She must need a hot beef injection to cure what ails her. Please insert said salami immediately.

☐ HUMMER

☐ **Definition:** Giving head, blowjob, BJ, going down, blowing the horn, deep throat, playing the pink oboe, playing the skin flute, breathing with the flesh snorkel, dining with Mr. One-Eye, outercourse, getting gobbled, scooby snack, lipstick on the dipstick, and yummy it down. Also known as fellatio, or oral stimulation of the male genitalia.

> **FUN FACTS!**
> *Most men consider a trip down south to be the absolute Holy Grail of sex acts. Why? Because the lips and tongue are warm, wet, soft, and awesome! Plus it's pure passive pleasure for the guy—all he does is lie back and enjoy.* ♂

☐ **Do you remember the first time I gave you a hummer?**

☐ **Hands-free? Hands-on? Slow? Fast? What techniques would you like for me to try?**

☐ **Should we take it to the next level? Mint? Ice cube? Whipped cream? Hum a tune?**

While the average summer sausage is 5.5 inches long, the average distance from mouth to throat is only 3.5, so "deep throating" is often quite uncomfortable. The good news is that the first 3 to 4 inches of the man meat have far greater concentrations of nerve endings than the rest of it, so focusing on what fits is best anyway. To protect against the dreaded gag, make a ring around the base with your fingers or hand. It feels great for him, and it allows you to control the depth of penetration.

BOOTY PRIZE
Good news! Your long wait has come to an end.
Pick a new prop—an Altoid perhaps?—and ask her to have at it!

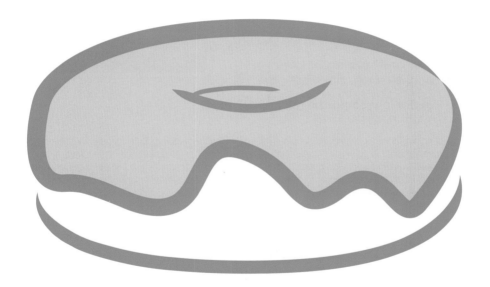

☐ **GLAZED DONUT**

☐ **Definition:** When a man goes for a little lunch downtown, below her equator, his face should resemble a glazed donut afterwards.

☐ **Do you like it when I go south with the mouth?**

☐ **What do you like best? Kissing, licking, lapping, sucking, blowing, nibbling?**

☐ **Would you like me to incorporate my hands? Toys?**

Like men, many women excitedly say that receiving the big lick is their favorite sexual pastime. Others report they are too shy to ask for it. The best way get started is with open communication. Talk about doing it, then go slow and ask her what she likes. Each woman is different, so what might have been orgasmic to someone else just might not do it for her. Try and ask as you lick along.

BOOTY PRIZE
He looks a little famished.
How about a box lunch?

☐ MONEY SHOT

☐ **Definition:** Chuck the custard, bust a nut, jizz, spooge, spunk, pop, blow a load, shoot the wad, climax, ejaculate. When a porn star does it on camera, it's called the money shot.

☐ **Do you wish you lasted longer? How can I help you stave off the point of no return?**

☐ **Which position is best for you to prolong the excitement?**

☐ **When the nut is busting, should I keep doing what I'm doing or stop? What about the afterglow? Cuddle, nap, or hamburger?**

Going from a two-pump chump to a stallion of stamina takes a lot of communication, patience, and practice. One strategy is increasing the strength of your PC muscles through Kegel exercises. Yes, men have PC muscles, too. You find them the same way a woman does. (See Beaver in chapter 1.) They are the muscles that stop and start your urine flow. The PC flutter is a Kegel exercise during which he contracts and relaxes the PC muscle over and over again. You know the PC is getting a good workout when it quivers or "flutters." It's like bench pressing for the johnson.

BOOTY PRIZE

Okay, guys, this shag session is all about you. Pick the position; dictate the action. But your "job" is to keep it going for at least 10 minutes. Are you up for the challenge?

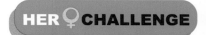

☐ THE BIG "O"

☐ **Definition:** Climax, come, fanny bomb, shake and shiver. The female orgasm.

☐ **What is the easiest way for you to have an "O"?**

☐ **Do you want to try another way? Can I try to give you multiples?**

☐ **Do you want to shoot for simultaneous Big O's?**

FUN FACTS!
It's not always about the hooha, boys! According to a 2009 survey, 75 percent of all women never reach orgasm from intercourse alone. Toys, hands, or tongue must get involved. So once again, do not forget about that little man in the boat.

Studies show that 2 out of 3 women have trouble reaching orgasm. That's a sad statistic, ladies. However, there is hope. All that is needed is a little change in the preplay. Additional studies have shown that with just 21 minutes of foreplay, this number changes to 9 out of 10 women who can achieve that euphoric state of pleasure.

BOOTY PRIZE
Think outside the "box"! Drive her to the Big O without penetration. It's all about her this time!

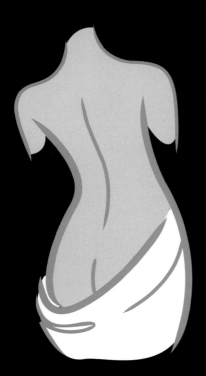
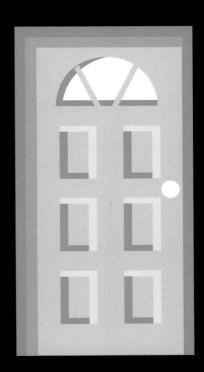

☐ GOING IN THE BACK DOOR

☐ **Definition:** Backdoor boogie, taking a trip to the moon, anal play.

☐ **Are you interested in exploring the back door?**

☐ **If so, should we start with a finger, a toy, or... well, you know?**

☐ **The back door swings both ways. Have you ever heard of bend-over boyfriends?**

> **FUN FACTS!**
> *Exit only? Due to its prevalence in Internet porn, interest in anal play has exploded. But proceed with caution! For many men and women, the back door is a no-fly zone, off limits to all intruders.*

Before boarding the caboose, it's important to go over a few ground rules. First, take it slow. Really slow. Start small, with a finger perhaps. Second, use lots of lube. Unlike the vajayjay, the rear entrance does not produce any natural lubrication, so lube it, and lube it good.

BOOTY PRIZE

You're back-door virgins? Discuss the possibility of a little anal play.
If you're both "bottoms up" for it, cut loose. Back-door veterans?
Take this opportunity to add some smooth new moves to your game.

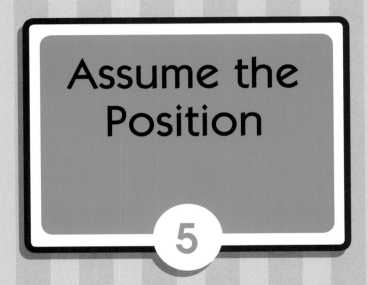

Assume the Position

5

☐ REVERSE COWGIRL

☐ **Definition:** Giddy up! A sexual position where the man lies on his back and the woman mounts him, facing his feet. The woman puts her hands on his hips and rides away!

☐ **Do you like it when I lean back?**

☐ **Do you like it when I move up and down or in circles?**

☐ **Should I wear my hat?**

Add some variety to her riding style! The frisky cowgirl can also recline to almost lying on the man's chest, offering him a great opportunity to reach in front of her to caress her body and provide bonus clitoral stimulation. Another sexy variation is for her to lean back and let her hair fall down and lightly sweep across his chest. For additional stimulation for him, try playing with his jewels while in this position.

BOOTY PRIZE
Yes, you are a stallion. Saddle up and let her ride!

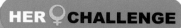

☐ SPORKING

☐ **Definition:** Why spoon when you can spork? Spooning is that lovely nonsexual cuddling that women enjoy so much. But when the guy's in back and inevitably throws wood, spooning becomes sporking.

☐ **How do you feel about a morning spork?**

☐ **Can I touch your little man in the boat at the same time?**

☐ **Want to try a variation? Lifting your leg? Intertwining our legs? With you lying on top of me?**

Spoons aligned in a kitchen drawer...lovers aligned in a cuddly embrace...Books have been written about spooning, but until now, sporking has been sadly ignored. Although not face-to-face, sporking is still quite intimate and it allows the woman to guide the man's hands to where she wants them. It's perfect for quiet, half-asleep morning sex and clandestine sex. Naked sporking offers head-to-toe skin contact and often results in a good ole forking.

BOOTY PRIZE

One sensual sporking session where he follows your rhythm and massages the bean.

☐ HEELS OVER HEAD

☐ **Definition:** A fun and exciting twist on the traditional missionary position. The woman lifts her legs so that her heels are above her head.

☐ **Does this position interest you?**

☐ **Should I spread my legs wide, scissors style, or keep my feet together?**

☐ **Would it turn you on if I wore my sexy high heels?**

Heels-over-head positions offer a number of exciting variations. To pleasure her passion pearl, have her spread her legs scissors style. For a tighter fit and oh-so-frantic friction, keep her ankles close together. Just remember to go slowly before you start thrusting away. If you thrust too hard and deep, you can hit her cervix, which can be painful. Easy, big boy!

BOOTY PRIZE
You're the director and costar of a movie called Heels Over Head. Ready, set, action! And there's no need to be quiet on the set.

☐ DOGGY STYLE

☐ **Definition:** Also known as rear entry and from behind; a sex position when the man is behind the woman, facing her backside and booty.

☐ **How should we position ourselves for a little rear-entry action? What's the best angle for you?**

☐ **How about a reach-around to flick my on-switch?**

☐ **I've been a naughty girl. How about a little spanking?**

Ladies, in addition to the dual pleasures of deep penetration and the beloved reach-around, rear entry positions can stimulate your G-spot like no other. To find your "Giddy up!" angle, change the position of your torso. You can lock your elbows, sit up so your back is against his chest, or lie down with your chest on a pillow. Once you have found the right angle for his dangle, tell him to stop the in-and-out while you sway your hips, grinding his glans into your G.

BOOTY PRIZE

*If you've done the doggy in the past, here's your chance to try a new variation.
Don't forget the reach-around!*

☐ **69**

☐ **Definition:** Two-can-chew, soixante-neuf, double lick, give-and-take, or simultaneous oral sex.

☐ **Should we shower before dining downtown?**

☐ **Which 69 position turns you on?**

☐ **Should I make you wait so we can crescendo together?**

Giving and receiving sexual pleasure at the same time is possibly the ultimate erotic sensation. Two-can-chew for mind-melting foreplay or the main event. Sixty-nine offers at least 4 position possibilities. The most common are woman on top, side by side, man on top and, if he's up for the challenge, standing. Variations and accessories can be used if 69 is uncomfortable due to major size differences between him and her. For instance, a Liberator wedge and ramp can help to modify the position if he is much taller.

BOOTY PRIZE
Try 3 of the position variations listed above.
Confer. Select a favorite. Repeat.

REVERSE WHEELBARROW

Definition: An acrobatic sex position where the woman wraps her arms around her standing man's neck and her legs around his waist. She then arches backward and rests her hands on the floor in a backbend position, while he supports her weight with his hands on her hips and bum.

What general flavor of acrobatic sex position intrigues you? Standing up? On a chair? In a swing?

Would you like to try the regular wheelbarrow first?

Is our health insurance paid up? Perhaps we should stretch a bit before commencing?

Hundreds of acrobatic sex positions are out there waiting to be discovered by the adventurous couple looking to spice up the daily routine. Yes, you want to try some crazy stuff, and, ladies, guys want to try it all. But you are not mind readers! You two must talk about what you want to try (or sometimes it's better to show and tell). Don't be shy. Go for it! Just don't forget to stretch.

BOOTY PRIZE

The cobra, the throne, the lotus, the spinner?
Choose a wild position that you'd both like to tackle.

☐ FROGGY STYLE

☐ **Definition:** In this woman-on-top position, she straddles him with a foot on either side of his hips like a frog and bounces up and down. She controls the rhythm and the angles for maximum pleasure.

☐ **Should I bounce gently or move in a circular motion? Both?**

☐ **What would you like to do with your hands while I'm froggying you?**

☐ **Do you like the view? Tell me more.**

Ladies, it's true. Year after year, guys report that woman-on-top positions are their absolute favorite. What's not to love? Great views, free hands, and you do all the work. Arch forward, lean backwards. Move in circles. Move up and down. Rotate. Tease and tantalize him by varying speed and depth. When you're on top, carnal creativity is a must!

BOOTY PRIZE
Hop on, girl! And while you're at it, make him beg for more!

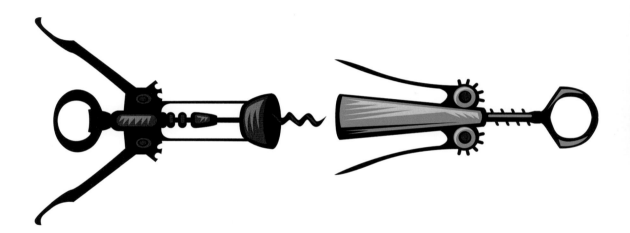

☐ THE CORKSCREW

☐ **Definition:** The woman is on her side with her legs bent towards her chest. She is lying on the edge of the bed or on a bench where he can stand or kneel. She opens her legs to let him enter her from behind and then closes them tightly.

☐ **Would you like to try it?**

☐ **How fast should I go?**

☐ **Should we try a different angle?**

FUN FACTS!
The corkscrew is a great position for stimulating your magic button. Don't worry about him, either; the frenulum friction will drive him into a frenzy. ♂

This position is unbelievably tight, so it is not about fast and deep thrusting. The corkscrew is about slow and controlled movements. Change the angle for a better view of one another, or vary the position to one where she is on her back with her legs together on either side of his shoulders.

BOOTY PRIZE
Try a variety of positions where her legs remain close together until you find the one that gives her the most clitoral stimulation. Meanwhile, enjoy the frenulum friction frenzy!

☐ REVERSE PIGGYBACK

☐ **Definition:** Imagine a man giving a woman a piggyback ride, but instead of riding on his back, she is riding on his front.

☐ **Do you like to stand and deliver?**

☐ **Tired? How about you lean me against the wall or put me down on the edge of the kitchen counter?**

☐ **Do you like it when I lock my legs around you?**

No one expects her boy to be Superman. If you are struggling to hold her up, make use of your basic household furniture. It is just as hot to use a wall for leverage or to carefully place her perfect derriere onto the desk or table. Another variation is to hold her bootylicious backside as she rests her feet on the bed, which she can also use for leverage for some bouncy action.

BOOTY PRIZE

No bedrooms available! One night of standing satisfaction incorporating 3 pieces of nonbedroom furniture.

Self-Love

6

☐ SPANK THE MONKEY

☐ **Definition:** Male masturbation, choking the chicken, flogging the dolphin, beating the meat, burping the baby, waxing the winkie, playing the skin flute…The list goes on and on and on.

☐ **What is your favorite term for spanking the monkey?**

☐ **Do you feel comfortable talking about massaging your member?**

☐ **How often do you play the skin flute?**

Unfortunately, self-love tends to get a bad rap. It is, in fact, a normal, healthy way to enjoy uncomplicated, safe, sexual pleasure. A man with a healthy and happy sex life may still masturbate on a regular basis. He may do it in private or in front of you. He could do it with his own thoughts or when looking at pictures or videos. Either way, self-love is a part of sexuality, and couples should make a point to discuss their feelings about it.

BOOTY PRIZE

One shopping trip for lubes, lotion, or any other monkey-spanking aid of his choice. Want some help? See "Sexy Slang Recommends" at the end of the book.

 *the*

☐ BUTTERING THE MUFFIN

☐ **Definition:** Caressing the kitty, airing the orchid, paddling the pink canoe, finger painting, dating the slick mitten, parting the pink sea, polishing the peanut, she-bop, shucking the oyster, or a night in with the girls. Otherwise known as female masturbation.

FUN FACTS!
A great way to get to know your body is by caressing it yourself. If you are familiar with what type of strokes or pressure works for you, then you will be able to communicate with him and guide him on this journey.

☐ **How do you feel about flying your Millennium Falcon with Hand Solo?**

☐ **Have you tried it?**

☐ **Would you be willing to do it in front of me so I can learn? (Really, it's all about the education.)**

Besides helping you to better communicate with your lover, a little kitty-caressing offers many benefits. It helps you to relax, can help you get a good night's sleep, and gives you sexual satisfaction at times when your lover might not be available.

BOOTY PRIZE
One shopping trip for lubes, lotions, toys, or any other muffin-buttering aid of her choice.

☐ ROSY PALM

☐ **Definition:** Another term for male self-love.

☐ **Do you like to use lubrication? What type?**

☐ **Where is your favorite place to have a date with Rosy Palm?**

☐ **Would you mind if I watched? I might want to join in!**

FUN FACTS!
Lubes are an excellent complement to a solo session. Stick with lubes made for sexual activity, if possible, and take caution when using common household options like soaps, shampoos, and lotions, some of which can irritate your skin and create a burning sensation in your little general's helmet. Choose your palm condiments wisely.

Besides your pal Rosy, a slew of devices are available to assist in your self-love sessions. Some are more elaborate than others, such as robotic mechanisms that simulate a hummer. One popular toy, the Glow Stroker, can be used solo or with your partner. It even glows in the dark!

BOOTY PRIZE
He picks the time and place to wax the winkie, and you enjoy the show.
You'll learn something new and then join in the fun.

☐ FLICKING THE BEAN

☐ **Definition:** Another term for female self-love.

☐ **Does watching sexy movies or reading sexy magazines and books turn you on?**

☐ **What do you think about when you push the pleasure button? What is your favorite fantasy?**

☐ **Do you want to try it with a toy?**

There is no official "right way" to polish the pearl. You can use your fingers, lube, toys, or even water from a showerhead. Be creative! Don't forget to pay attention to the thoughts that turn you on. Fantasize, read erotic fiction, check out a sexy series on "Skinemax." Flicking the bean is normal and natural. It's a great way to experiment and find what works best for you. The more you know what turns you on, both mentally and physically, the more satisfaction you will gain from a steamy session with your boy toy.

BOOTY PRIZE
Boys! Pay attention! Watch and learn as she airs the orchid.
When SHE is ready, you'll be invited to visit the garden of delight.

No,
It's Not a Back
Massager

7

☐ POCKET ROCKET

☐ **Definition:** A discreet, compact-sized vibrator used on its own or in conjunction with other sexual activity. Primarily used for external clitoral stimulation, this little buzzing buddy can work miracles.

FUN FACTS!
A pocket rocket is proof that things don't have to be large to get the job done!

☐ **Have you ever used an "adult" toy?**

☐ **If so, what is your favorite?**

☐ **If no, would you like to try one? Do you want to try it together or alone?**

Many men are intimidated by vibrators, afraid that the woman might desire the vibrator more than the man. Don't be intimidated, boys! A vibrator can make your life easier. They increase sexual responsiveness in most females and help get their motor running. If both of you are new to the adult toy department, try to steer clear of the monstrous double-headed vibrating strap-on, which will only frighten you. Start small with something like a pocket rocket, egg, or bullet.

BOOTY PRIZE
One session of vibrating pleasure where you show him how to use it on you. Your batteries are rechargeable, right?

☐ VIBRATING LOVE RING 🐓

☐ **Definition:** Also known as a vibrating ring, this sex toy consists of a stretchable, circular ring of silicone with one (or even two) small vibrators attached. The ring is put on the base of the erect penis with the mini-vibe on top. It's designed to stimulate the clitoris during intercourse. Turn on the love ring, and you both will be turned on!

> **FUN FACTS!**
> *Sex toys for men? Seems unnecessary or redundant, doesn't it? But, by restricting blood flow out of the little general, a vibrating love ring can thicken and firm the python while simultaneously stimulating her love button. Yes, it's a win-win proposition.* ♂

☐ **Would you like to experience a vibrating love ring?**

☐ **How does it feel? Does the vibrator turn you on?**

☐ **Would you like to rotate the ring and try a different position?**

Dozens of brand names and variations are available, and many are packaged with a condom. Vibrating rings are a great "starter" toy. Just slide it on, turn it on, and knock boots.

BOOTY PRIZE
Shop together for a buzzing-bits bauble. She's buying! (You're in luck, girls. Most vibrating love rings cost less than $20, and we've helped you narrow down the choices. See "Sexy Slang Recommends" at the end of the book.)

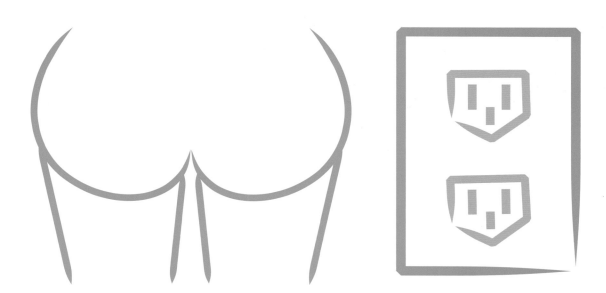

☐ BUM PLUG

☐ **Definition:** A sex toy that is inserted into the chocolate starfish.

☐ **Does the thought of using a butt plug intrigue you?**

☐ **Are you interested in giving, receiving, or both?**

☐ **What are your concerns or fears about using backdoor toys?**

> **FUN FACTS!**
> *A variety of toys for the bum are available, but butt plugs are specifically shaped to give a feeling of fullness in the back door. They are not intended to be moved in and out. When used during the main event, a plug increases the stimulation of the G-spot in a woman and, for a man, it stimulates his prostate.*

Toys for the tush come in a variety of colors, shapes, sizes, and textures, and with multiple features to accommodate any experience level. They can be a great way to introduce anal play into a relationship. Only use toys designed for this particular region, and have plenty of lube on hand. Most are created with a flared base so they don't end up stuck somewhere you don't want them to be. The proper care and washing of bum toys is also very important. Anything going in the back door and coming out again cannot be readmitted without a proper and thorough cleaning.

BOOTY PRIZE

Plug it in? Your choice. If not in the back door, then how about a new toy for the front?

☐ FURRY HANDCUFFS

☐ **Definition:** A fuzzy implement of "light bondage" used to restrict a person's movement. In hard-core bondage, the "top" applies the handcuffs and the "bottom" is restrained. You always wondered; now you know.

☐ **Furry handcuffs? Light bondage? Us? Seriously? Are we willing to give it a try?**

☐ **Do you want to be the "top" or the "bottom"? Who goes first?**

☐ **What if the bottom is uncomfortable? Should we have a safety word like "tapioca" or "paleontology"?**

Worry not. Fooling around with furry handcuffs doesn't mean you're on the pulpy road to leather hoods and bullwhips. Many carefree couples report that light bondage enhances their sex lives, freeing them from their normal inhibitions. Using furry handcuffs is a safe and hopefully enjoyable visit to the wild side.

BOOTY PRIZE
Step One: Buy furry handcuffs. (Or take them out of your goodie drawer.)
Step Two: Take turns being the top and the bottom. It's your booty prize, tough guy, so you choose who goes first.

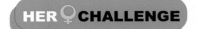

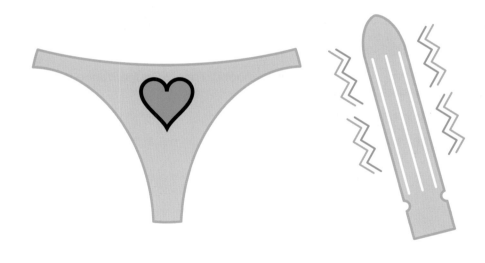

☐ REMOTE-CONTROL PANTY VIBRATOR

☐ **Definition:** What mad genius invented these boisterous bloomers? A pair of women's underwear with a secret pocket holding a small vibrator that can be turned on with a wireless remote control from up to 20 feet away.

> **FUN FACTS!**
> *Exciting for voyeurs (him) and adventurous exhibitionists (you), these pulsating pantaloons leave wearers panting. But buyers beware! They vary widely in quality and price.*
>
> ♀

☐ **Want to try them? Where? Romantic dinner? On the dance floor? Seventh inning of a baseball game?**

☐ **Do you trust me with the remote?**

☐ **Is it possible to have a discreet orgasm in public?**

Fans of these nasty knickers enjoy the thrill of danger, suspense, and surprise. When will he flip the switch? The anticipation alone is such a thrill that users report not being able to wait.

BOOTY PRIZE
An entire evening where you are actually excited to give him the remote control.

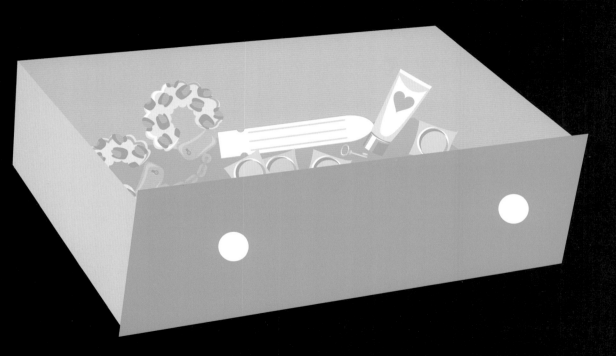

☐ GOODIE DRAWER

☐ **Definition:** The secret assortment of sex toys, lubes, condoms, lotions, candles, spare batteries, and other erotic accoutrements that every woman has (or should have). Analogous to the male porn stash.

☐ **Did you know I have (or don't have) a goodie drawer?**

☐ **What's your favorite item in my treasure chest?**

☐ **What's missing from my goodie drawer?**

In Sex and the City, *when Charlotte commented that she didn't have a goodie drawer, a shocked Samantha exclaimed, "I have a goodie closet!" Whether you have closet or a shoebox, make sure it's well-stocked with your—and his—favorite things.*

BOOTY PRIZE
Choose one item from her horny hoard, or add an item to it. Become an expert at its use. Practice makes perfect!

Walk on the Wild Side

8

☐ SHRIMPING

☐ **Definition:** A sexual fetish involving the licking or sucking of the distal phalanges, aka, the toes.

☐ Do you want to try shrimping?

☐ What fetishes gross you out? What fetishes turn you on?

☐ Is there another part of your body that I should be licking and sucking?

> **FUN FACTS!**
> *Podophilia, better known as a "foot fetish," is the most common sexual fetish. Recently, rock star Sting was photographed sucking his wife's toes on a yacht in Sydney Harbor.*

A fetish is defined as something—such as a material object or a nonsexual part of the body—that arouses sexual desire. Many men get turned on from the faint glimpse of a bra strap or a tan line; some get aroused from the mere whiff of brownies or the sound of the ocean. Get to know your partner's fetishes, and use them to attract and entice.

BOOTY PRIZE
If you don't want to give him a full serving of shrimp, then how about having him give you a relaxing foot massage?

FRENCH MAID OUTFIT

Definition: A costume worn by a woman for the purpose of sexy role-playing. Other familiar fantasy outfits include doctor or nurse, cheerleader or quarterback, schoolgirl, construction worker, and Tarzan or Jane.

Do you have a favorite role-playing fantasy? Can I guess before you tell me?

What costumes or props should we acquire?

Should we stay in character—"keep it real," as the pros say—or just have fun with it?

Couples often find role-playing more exciting away from home. Spend a weekend at the beach and let the sexy lifeguard "rescue" you. Or sneak into the office on a Saturday and get "serviced" by your secretary. The possibilities are limited only by your imagination. Acting out fantasies can broaden your horizons and deepen your relationship.

BOOTY PRIZE

What will it be, gentleman? Stripper and client? Photographer and model? Don't be shy; she's game for a little play. Just make sure it has more than one act!

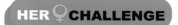

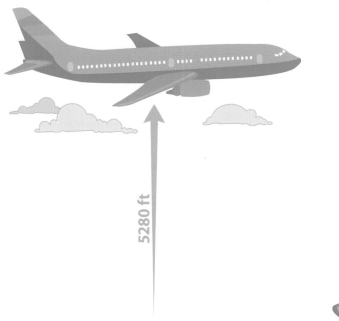

5280 ft

☐ MILE HIGH CLUB

☐ **Definition:** If you have engaged in sexual intercourse on an airplane while in flight, congratulations! You and your partner are members of the Mile High Club.

☐ **Does the thought of joining the Mile High Club turn you on?**

☐ **What about going at it in another unusual or public place? Any fantasies you'd like to fulfill?**

☐ **What if we get caught? What will we say to stay out of trouble?**

Fear? Embarrassment? Perhaps the biggest barrier to joining the club is the tiny, disgusting restrooms found on most airplanes. But if you're bound and determined to punch your membership card, your best bet would be to go for it on a red-eye, and by "red-eye" we mean an overnight flight, not your one-eyed trouser snake. Another option: Consider paying for it. On special charter flights, the mile-high mattress dance won't land you in jail.

BOOTY PRIZE

Choose a different and possibly unusual location to get it on. Whether you pick a public park, a plane, your patio, or simply your kitchen counter, the goal is to mix it up!

□ PRINCE ALBERT

□ **Definition:** The most common male genital piercing, a circular ring enters through the urethral opening and pierces the penis, emerging from the frenulum on the underside of the wounded warrior. Ouch!

□ **Body piercings: hot or not?**

□ **What about clip-on jewelry? Get the look without the permanence and pain.**

□ **Do you want to try anything else that's categorized as "kinky"?**

> **FUN FACTS!**
> *Men who have survived the Prince Albert—and many of the women who love them—report that the pierced penis enhances sexual pleasure. Others say the "kinky" factor stimulates the mind more than the body.*

The history of the Prince Albert is debated, but some scholars believe it's named after Queen Victoria's husband, who had his penis pierced to avoid a bulge while wearing the incredibly tight trousers that were the fashion of the time. A hook on the inside of the trousers would hold the damaged dangler in place via the "dressing ring." Talk about a slave to fashion!

BOOTY PRIZE

A piercing perhaps, real or faux? Or maybe something leather or latex? High-heeled stilettos? If you've ever wanted to indulge your "kinky" side, here's your chance!

☐ CLUB SANDWICH

☐ **Definition:** Ménage à trois, threesome, three-way, the Big 3. A type of group sex involving 3 people.

☐ **Have you ever fantasized about threesomes? Tell me about it.**

☐ **Do you have any other group-sex fantasies? The classic Roman orgy, perhaps?**

☐ **Should we discuss acting out one of our fantasies? What rules would we establish?**

Often fantasies do not live up to expectations. Building a club sandwich in your boudoir can open a Pandora's box of resentment and jealousy that can poison your relationship faster than you can say "pass the lube." So proceed cautiously if you both fantasize about it. Plenty of discussion and unbreakable ground rules are absolutely necessary.

BOOTY PRIZE
Share your favorite fantasy story and ask him to do the same. If you don't have one, make one up. Be creative. Sexy stories often lead to new experiences.

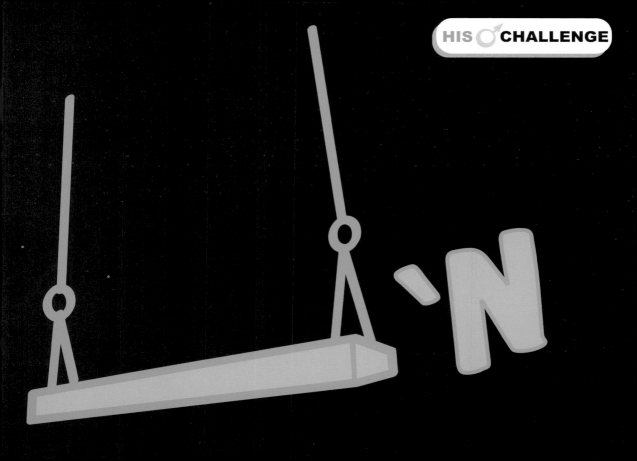

□ SWINGING

□ **Definition:** Also known as wife swapping and "the lifestyle." When couples swap partners for sexual pleasure, they're swinging.

□ **How do feel about "the lifestyle"? Have you known any swingers?**

□ **Have you ever been hit on by a couple?**

□ **Forget the partner swap. How about a romp on the backyard swing set?**

FUN FACTS!
The North American Swing Club Association estimates that 5 million swingers are active in the United States. Several hundred clubs nationwide cater to these couples, and the Lifestyles Organization, which hosts an annual convention in Las Vegas (big surprise!), recently celebrated its 35th anniversary. ♂

Whether you choose to swap or not, just talking about your fantasies can spice up your sex life. Forty-four percent of couples who talk about their fantasies label their sex lives "very exciting," compared with only 28 percent of those who don't share their fantasies with each other.

BOOTY PRIZE
She is the star in your fantasy come to life. Choreograph the action, and enjoy the wild ride!

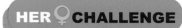

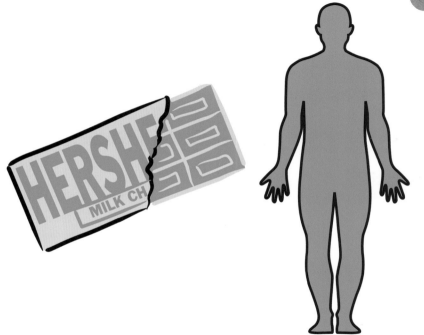

☐ CHOCOLATE BODY PAINT

☐ **Definition:** Edible body paints come in a variety of flavors, including chocolate, cherry, vanilla, and even green apple. Strip down, paint in on, and lick it off. Yum!

☐ **Are you "hungry"? Do we have anything in the fridge that might satisfy your carnal craving?**

☐ **What's your favorite aphrodisiac?**

☐ **What part of my body would you like to butter up? How about yourself?**

Don't wait 9½ weeks to lick something delicious off your lover's sweet spots. Food foreplay is playful, fun, and nutritious!

BOOTY PRIZE
You're the gourmet today. Ravish him with your own special recipe.

☐ BALL COLLAR

☐ **Definition:** A ring or bracelet-like device, typically made of leather or rubber, that is slipped over the testicles and tightened above them, often for the purpose of inflicting pain.

☐ **Does the idea of giving or receiving a little pain interest you? Why or why not?**

☐ **How about spanking?**

☐ **Riding crops? Ball gags? Blindfolds? Paddles? Should we visit a store and check it all out?**

> **FUN FACTS!**
> *You've heard the term "S&M," right? It's short for sadomasochism, a consensual sexual practice during which one person inflicts pain on another. The "S" in the S&M twosome gives the pain, and the "M" submits to it.* ♂

Gentle spanking is the most common form of S&M. Few people who give the tush a love tap consider themselves sadists. More intense S&M practices include flagellation (whipping) and dripping hot wax.

BOOTY PRIZE

If together you've graduated from the furry handcuffs in chapter 7 and are ready, willing, and able to kick it up a notch, here's your chance. But remember, in this case it's not always better to give than to receive—take turns being a top and a bottom.

☐ SURFING THE CRIMSON WAVE

☐ **Definition:** Getting it on with Aunt Flo. Parting the Red Sea. Sex during menstruation.

☐ Do you get horny during your period?

☐ Are you comfortable having sex during this time, or do you fear it grosses me out?

☐ Maybe sex in the shower is a more appealing option?

FUN FACTS!
Thanks to flaring hormones, many women report extreme horniness while flying the red flag. And there's no physical reason the road must be closed for repairs, so give the lady what she wants!

Doing the horizontal mambo during that time of the month has its benefits. Orgasm can reduce cramps (hers, big guy, not yours), and a recent study found that surfing the crimson wave lowers the risk of endometriosis. No kidding! So if you feel the need, don't surrender to the red flag.

BOOTY PRIZE

If Aunt Flo is cramping your style, the doctor is in the house. Pick your prescription: a back massage, a front massage, or just some nice, gentle spooning.

☐ SHOCKER

☐ **Definition:** Two in the beaver, one checking her fever. Two in the bush, one in the tush. Two in the pink, one in the stink. Two in the clam, one in the shazaam! We're talking about simultaneously inserting the index and middle fingers into the vagina and the "pinky" finger into the anus.

☐ How about that shocker?

☐ Which foreplay moves do you enjoy the most? What would you like to do more of? Less of?

☐ Is it actually possible for a man to engage in 20 minutes of foreplay?

Tantalizing the tush while pleasuring the pink palace can add an erotic new sensation, leading to an intense orgasm. But do not shock her with the shocker! Communicate your intentions and respond to her nonverbal signals. And, one more time, slow down. Foreplay isn't all that bad, is it?

BOOTY PRIZE

Yes, gentlemen, this is your prize. Enjoy at least 20 minutes of steamy foreplay. When you both can't wait, consummate.

☐ TOSSED SALAD

☐ **Definition:** Licking or probing the anus with the tongue, also known as rimming, cleaning the kitchen, and analingus.

☐ **Are you intrigued with the notion of giving or receiving a tossed salad?**

☐ **Have you ever heard of a rusty trombone?**

☐ **If cleaning the kitchen's not on the menu, what new frisky activity would you like to try?**

FUN FACTS!
No body part is saddled with more social taboos than the super-sensitive anus, which means that some people find anal play to be an exciting, naughty thrill. If this doesn't describe you, that's fine too.

♀

Safety first! If you are intrigued by the salad but are concerned about hygiene and safety, consider using a dental dam. It allows the same stimulation and even comes in flavors like vanilla and wildberry!

BOOTY PRIZE
He will clean the kitchen, either figuratively or literally.

128

Respect and Protect Yourself

9

☐ LOVE GLOVE

☐ **Definition:** Safety first! No glove, no love! A love glove is a sheath-like covering for a johnson to protect against pregnancy and sexually transmitted diseases. Sometimes referred to as a raincoat or "Mr. Happy's business suit" but most widely known as a condom.

☐ **How do you feel about wearing a raincoat? Does it change the feeling?**

☐ **Would you like me to put it on, or would you like to do it?**

☐ **Do you like it better with lubrication or without?**

With so many shapes and sizes these days, one is sure to "suit" your needs. Don't be afraid to try a variety. Remember, practice makes perfect! The most common complaint about condoms is that putting them on is a mood killer. Make sure that you are both familiar with the packaging of your favorites so you don't get caught in that "How the heck do I open this thing?" situation in the heat of the moment.

BOOTY PRIZE
Shop and score! 1. Go on a shopping spree together and choose a variety of styles. 2. Proceed to test each one and give it a score. 3. Pick your favorite. 4. Repeat the test (just to make sure).

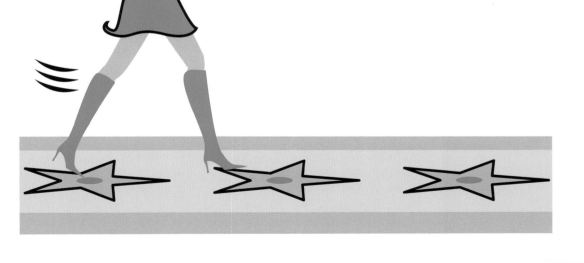

☐ WALK OF FAME

☐ **Walk of Shame Definition:** Waking up in a unfamiliar bed, trapped under an unfamiliar arm, with a blazing hangover, and then trying to scramble into your clothes and stumble your way back home in heels and last night's dress as you recall the bizarre and fuzzy moments of the night before.

☐ **Walk of Fame Definition:** Waking up, rolling over, and smiling with enthusiasm about your bed companion and last night's "activities."

☐ **What do you like to do immediately after experiencing the hot beef injection?**

☐ **Do you like to be held? Kissed? Touched?**

☐ **Is there anything you would like to hear from me other than snoring or "Do you want to go again?"**

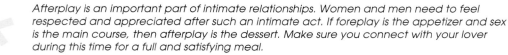

Afterplay is an important part of intimate relationships. Women and men need to feel respected and appreciated after such an intimate act. If foreplay is the appetizer and sex is the main course, then afterplay is the dessert. Make sure you connect with your lover during this time for a full and satisfying meal.

BOOTY PRIZE

One afterplay session where you call the shots.

☐ BUN IN THE OVEN

☐ **Definition:** Preggers, pregnant, knocked up, expecting, incubating, showing the baby bump.

☐ How do you feel about sex during pregnancy?

☐ What position would best turn you on?

☐ What is your favorite thing about pregnant women? Do you want to try some hot Demi Moore–style photography?

Without a doubt, a bun in the oven will bring about some changes in your sex life, many of which are for the better. The experience of parenthood can strengthen a couple's bond and make intimacy much more enjoyable. Also, due to her changing size and comfort level, you will be inclined to try out some new positions. You never know what might end up in your regular romping repertoire! Be sure to understand and communicate with one another during all the stages of pregnancy (and post-baby, too) so you can continue with the lusty scenes that got you the bun in the first place.

BOOTY PRIZE

Doctors require post-baby couples to wait a number of weeks before resuming the main event. During that time, you are sure to need a release. Now is a great opportunity for her to practice her "everything but" techniques.

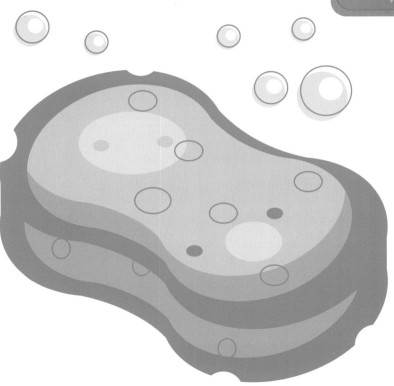

THE SPONGE

Definition: Shaped like a small disc of spongy foam, the sponge is inserted into a woman's vajayjay and provides 3 methods of contraceptive protection against his determined swimmers. Unlike birth control pills, the sponge is nonhormonal and is only used when needed.

Is he spongeworthy?

What methods of birth control are you interested in using?

What methods do you not want to use?

Patches, pills, rings, shots, sponges, and caps. A myriad of methods are available to men and women for contraception. Talk to your significant other and investigate which method(s) work best for both of you. And don't forget that many methods offer additional benefits such as improved complexion, reduced cramps, and, most importantly, disease protection.

BOOTY PRIZE
So now you're protected—what are you waiting for?

☐ BEDABLE

☐ **Definition:** Worthy of sex.

☐ **What made me bedable?**

☐ **What was the most memorable thing about our first time?**

☐ **Am I worthy of another romp?**

Being bedable does not start in the boudoir. The little things can make a woman hot for you. Surprise her by picking up her favorite flowers, music, or food. Pamper her; tell her how pretty, wonderful, smart, and amazing she is. For a man, the little things, such as breathing, can make him want you. However, you could add some spicy lingerie, provocative talk, or a sexy flash of cleavage. The point is to always make an effort to be bedable.

BOOTY PRIZE
One sultry seduction session by her until you deem her bedable. Try to hold out for more than 2 minutes, boys.

Random Acts
of Playfulness

10

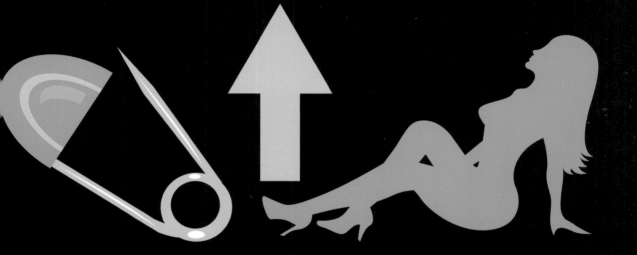

☐ PIN-UP GIRL

☐ **Definition:** An iconic image in American pop culture and the precursor of modern pornography. Mass-produced images of beautiful women have been popular since the 1890s. From Betty Grable to Farrah Fawcett to Cindy Crawford, pin-up girls are every boy's fantasy.

☐ What was your first encounter with a pin-up girl? The first time you saw a *Playboy*? Something more hard-core?

☐ Did you have any posters on your wall or pictures in your school locker?

☐ What erotic images turn you on? Care to share?

Today, erotic images—and, many would argue, pornography—are unavoidable. From cable television to the Internet to spam email, Americans are inundated with what used to be available only on a few cave walls. Being visual creatures, men typically respond to films and photos of nekkid ladies, while women often find erotic tales more titillating. Read a tale and get some tail? Sounds like a fair trade!

BOOTY PRIZE
Time for show-and-tell! Show her an item from your erotic collection, and tell her what you like about it or what you'd like to try.

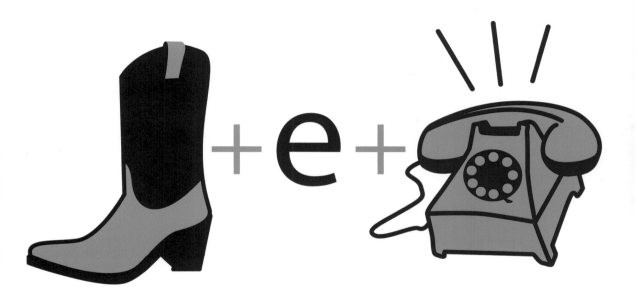

☐ BOOTY CALL

☐ **Definition:** Phoning a person for the sole purpose of hooking up. You can either give a booty call or be considered a booty call if you are the recipient of such a call.

☐ **Shall we pick a code word for sex so we can keep our booty calls and texts private from wandering eyes and ears?**

☐ **Would it turn you on if I texted you that I was in a various state of undress? Braless? Pantyless?**

☐ **Our code word or phrase? How about we incorporate names for our favorite body parts? Mr. Johnson is hungry for a whisker biscuit?**

As a couple, you can have a lot of fun with the booty call, the perfect mechanism with which to flirt and flatter. If you are out with the girls, booty call him with a message that you expect him waiting in bed, pantless, upon your arrival home. If you're together at a crowded party, text her from across the room with a message that she looks smoking hot tonight. Think of how excited he will be when he's out with the guys watching sports and all of a sudden he receives a text to meet you in the shower, pronto!

BOOTY PRIZE
Your text wish is his command. Hit that keyboard with a randy request, girl!

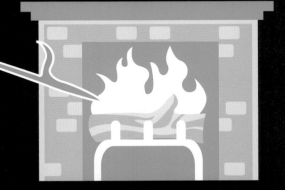

☐ SOAK AND POKE

☐ **Definition:** A bathtub large enough for two people. You soak, and, since you're already naked, you poke. H_2Oooooh!

☐ **How about a bubble bath? Or a soapy shower?**

☐ **Shall we go all the way, or move to our den of love for the hibbidy-dibbidy?**

☐ **What accessories might we want for our erotic visit to Wet & Wild?**

Because water washes away a woman's natural lubrication, underwater action can be H_2Ouch! instead of H_2Oooooh. But don't despair…dozens of soak-safe sex toys are available, including waterproof vibrators. Silicone-based lubricants also stay slick in water, and, unlike oil-based lubes, silicone is condom-safe.

BOOTY PRIZE
Soak or shower, your choice. If she's feeling wild and wet, poke.

☐ NOONER

☐ **Definition:** Midday intercourse, often time challenged, in which case it's a "quickie."

☐ **Should we schedule a nooner?**

☐ **Where should we enjoy our frantic frolic? Lock the office door?**

☐ **Do you have any quickie fantasies, like love in an elevator?**

FUN FACTS!
A libidinous lunch break may be just what you need in the middle of a stressful day, according to experts. Add an element of danger to the mix, like doing it in the backseat of your car, and you'll really drive him wild. But please, ladies, no quickie jokes like "Aren't they always quickies?"

A nooner can be fast, or it can be slow. The point is not the pace but the timing. Afternoon delight is a slice of forbidden fruit, an opportunity to play hooky from work or family obligations. If it's going to be a clothes-on quickie, a little lube might help. Also it's a good idea to get in the mood mentally. Think about it. Picture the passion. Get excited!

BOOTY PRIZE

Many people think nooners are all about him, but not this time. You pick the hour and place, and whether it's a leisurely gourmet meal or feverish fast food, you call the shots.

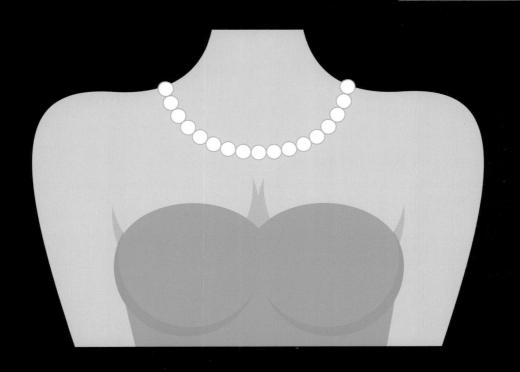

☐ PEARL NECKLACE

☐ **Definition:** The "off-shoot" or end result of hooter humping. A man's trouser snake slithers between the twins, which are squeezed together. A little back-and-forth commences. When he ejaculates, the sinewy splash of spooge that gathers around her neck and shoulder blades resembles a pearl necklace.

☐ **Do you love my love pillows? Tell me more.**

☐ **Honey, would you like to do my melons?**

☐ **While we're on the subject of pearl necklaces, shall we visit a jewelry store together one day soon?**

Sometimes, for one reason or another, the vajayjay needs a break. Aunt Flo might be paying a visit, or it's a postpartum medical necessity. When "everything but" is the only option, you have many options!

BOOTY PRIZE

Go ahead. Have some fun, and bejewel those beautiful begonias!

☐ DIRTY DANCING

☐ **Definition:** Grinding, freaking, pole dancing, lap dance, the forbidden dance, you name it. If it gets you hot, then it's dirty dancing.

☐ Can you show me how to bump and grind with you?

☐ Would you like for me to give you a little striptease?

☐ Will you give me one?

Exotic dancing is not just her domain, boys. You can perform a variety of sexy dance moves for her. The key thing to remember is have fun with it. She doesn't expect you to be a Vegas Chippendale—just laugh with her and try out new things. You never know what kind of heat your gyrations will generate.

BOOTY PRIZE
Let's see his freak flag fly! He gives you a five-minute performance of exotic and erotic dance moves.

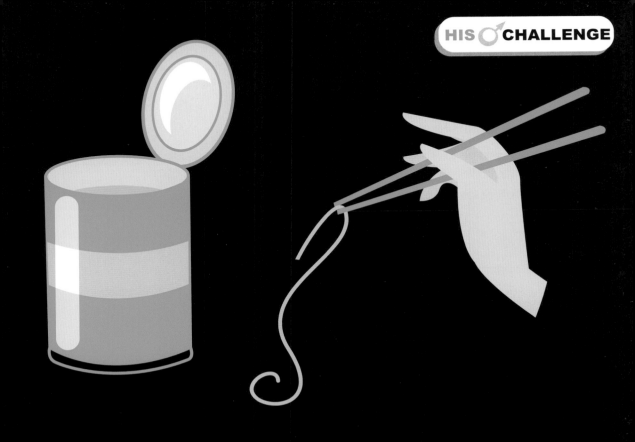

☐ CANOODLE

☐ **Definition:** PDA (public display of affection). Kissing, snuggling, and petting...in public.

☐ **Do you want to canoodle with me? What do you think is appropriate PDA?**

☐ **Does it turn you on to see others in a session of hot and heavy petting?**

☐ **Would it turn you on if I offered you a little indecent exposure?**

Canoodling and exhibitionism can be fun and exhilarating, whether you're getting a little booty in the parents' house or providing a little covert under-the-tablecloth massage of his manhood at a restaurant. Either way, just make sure you have a plan of action if you get caught. Unless of course, you want to be...

BOOTY PRIZE

She's a trench-coat temptress! Watch as she performs a titillating act of exhibitionism for you. Enjoy!

> **FUN FACTS!**
> *You may be familiar with canoodling from popular gossip columns like the New York Post's "Page Six"..."So-and-so starlet was last seen canoodling with a hot unnamed hunk in an East Village bar, much to her boy toy's dismay..."*

☐ DIRTY TALK

☐ **Definition:** When sweet nothings turn into suggestive, salacious, sexual somethings, it's dirty talk.

☐ **Can I talk dirty to you?**

☐ **What words do you not like to hear? What words most turn you on?**

☐ **What do you want to say to me right now?**

Discussing "talk" is a great way to end this book! There is a fine line between when to use sweet slang or downright dirty slang or even proper terminology. We created this book to make sexy topics lighthearted and fun. Be sure to communicate—talk and listen—with your lover about what turns you both on. Open and honest communication is the best way to grow and strengthen a lasting relationship.

BOOTY PRIZE

Using no-holds-barred dirty talk, whisper in her ear what you would like to do to her and then proceed with action to back up those words!

Sexy Slang
Recommends

Many of the Challenges and Booty Prizes suggest you shop together for new "toys" and other goodie drawer items and, to get the most from this book and truly spice up your sex life, you should do just that!

 For **shopping suggestions** and **discounts**, go to our website
www.sexyslang.com/bedroomchallenges.html

In order to make it less intimidating, we have handpicked our favorites and worked out special deals when possible. You can find these recommendations and special deals on **www.sexyslang.com/bedroomchallenges.html.**

Other SEXY SLANG Products

Our party game that started it all! Sexy Slang has 500 terms that players must race to act out or draw. Perfect for dinner parties, game nights, or bachelorettes, Sexy Slang will make you laugh until it hurts!

Our charades-only version of Sexy Slang. It contains 300 titillating terms and travels well, so it's perfect for that vacation house.

> Couples Who
> Play Together
> STAY TOGETHER!
> Visit us at
> **WWW.SEXYSLANG.COM**

A full-sized dart board featuring 20 sex positions as well as traditional numbers. Play regular darts or Sexy Slang's naughty version, including "Carnal Cricket," "69," and "You Just Can't Lose!"

Games

Apparel

Sexy Slang Tees showcase fun and flirty terms from the Sexy Slang games. Flatter that special someone with a "Chick Magnet" or an "Eye Candy" tee.

Many more designs available at
www.sexyslang.com

Sexy Slang Tees are hilarious icebreakers. Choose from a variety of G-rated to R-rated designs. Available at **www.sexyslang.com** as well as Walmart, Kohl's, and many other retailers.

stud

Search "Sexy Slang" in the iTunes store or go to **www.sexyslang.com**

Sexy Slang's Bachelorette Challenge iPhone App
Get the bachelorette party started with this hilarious, interactive game for the bachelorette and her entourage to play while out on the town. She is sure to have an unforgettable night with these sexy and outrageous challenges.

Sexy Slang's Naughty & Nice Charades iPhone App
Now you can download Sexy Slang's Naughty Charades board game! If you are looking for a last minute way to spice up your next party, then this is the app for you.

iPhone Apps

Accessories

Sexy Slang Accessories include iPhone, laptop, and guitar hero skins, posters, postcards, guitar accessories, and many more! Info at **www.sexyslang.com**

And introducing our new, family-friendly brand

New products based on Sports Slang. Info at **www.sportyslang.com**

Bonus Challenges & Booty Prizes

We hope you enjoyed Sexy Slang's Bedroom Challenges, but finishing the book is only the beginning! Yes, there's more!

 Go to our website **www.sexyslang.com/bedroomchallenges.html**

Here you will find bonus challenges and booty prizes as well as opportunities to participate in contests. You can also add your comments and feedback for upcoming Sexy Slang books, games, and apparel.

Get Social!

Become a Fan on Facebook
Receive special Sexy Slang discounts and participate in weekly contests.
www.facebook.com/sexyslang

Follow Sexy Slang on Twitter
Follow Sexy Slang authors on Twitter for fun contests and info on keeping life sexy.
www.twitter.com/sexyslang

Read Sexy Slang's Blog
Learn about the hilarious escapades encountered when you are a sexy product entrepreneur.
http://site.sexyslang.com/blog

Watch Sexy Slang on YouTube
Check out the wild Sexy Slang on the street videos and see what other people said
when asked questions from Sexy Slang's Bedroom Challenges.
www.youtube.com/sexyslang

Do you know what Sexy Slang saying this picture represents?
Find the answer at **www.sexyslang.com/bedroomchallenges.html**

About the Authors

Christi Smith Scofield and Ted Scofield are the creators of the Sexy Slang brand with products for sale in more than five thousand stores across the country. They (or their products) have been featured by a diverse assortment of national media, including CNBC, *ABC Nightly News*, Fox News, *CW News*, *AM New York*, *The Montel Williams Show*, *BusinessWeek*, *Cosmopolitan*, *Self*, *Redbook*, *Playboy*, *Ebony*, *Better TV*, *Village Voice*, *Crain's New York Business*, and Cosmo Radio.

Christi graduated with a BA in business from Virginia Wesleyan College, where she was captain of the soccer team and, go figure, her sorority's social chair. While working as a sales manager in the technology industry, she earned an MBA from Florida State University. Ted is a three-time graduate of Vanderbilt University, earning a BA, MBA, and JD. Christi and Ted live in New York City and have started work on a second Sexy Slang book.